Strange Land

University of Central Florida Contemporary Poetry Series

Florida A&M University, Tallahassee
Florida Atlantic University, Boca Raton
Florida Gulf Coast University, Ft. Myers
Florida International University, Miami
Florida State University, Tallahassee
University of Central Florida, Orlando
University of Florida, Gainesville
University of North Florida, Jacksonville
University of South Florida, Tampa
University of West Florida, Pensacola

Poetry by Sharon Kraus
Generation
Strange Land

Strange Land

Sharon Kraus

University Press of Florida

Gainesville · Tallahassee · Tampa · Boca Raton

Pensacola · Orlando · Miami · Jacksonville · Ft. Myers

07 06 05 04 03 02   6 5 4 3 2 1

Library of Congress Cataloging-in-Publication Data
Kraus, Sharon, 1961–
Strange land / Sharon Kraus.
p. cm.—(University of Central Florida contemporary poetry series)
ISBN 0-8130-2449-8 (cloth: alk. paper)
ISBN 0-8130-2450-1 (pbk.: alk. paper)
I. Title. II. Contemporary poetry series (Orlando, Fla.)
PS3561.R2884 S87 2002
811'.54—dc21   2001054051

The University Press of Florida is the scholarly publishing agency
for the State University System of Florida, comprising Florida A&M
University, Florida Atlantic University, Florida Gulf Coast University,
Florida International University, Florida State University, University of
Central Florida, University of Florida, University of North Florida,
University of South Florida, and University of West Florida.

University Press of Florida
15 Northwest 15th Street
Gainesville, FL 32611–2079
http://www.upf.com

for Brian Murphy,
sine quo non

Contents

Acknowledgments

Grateful acknowledgment is made to the editors of the following journals, in which some of the poems in this book originally appeared: *Barrow Street, Cortland Review, ForPoetry.com, The Massachusetts Review*, ONTHEBUS, *Poet Lore, Puerto del Sol*, and *Salamander*.

"Fractals" originally appeared in *The Georgia Review* 53, no. 4 (Winter 1999), copyright 1999 by The University of Georgia. Reprinted by permission of *The Georgia Review.*

"The Measure" was first published in *Quarterly West* 50 (2000).

With thanks to the MacDowell Colony for residencies which allowed me to complete this book.

For their unyielding support and generous discernment, I thank Audrey Alenson, Elizabeth Andrews, Ralph Black, Julie Carr, Shira Dentz, Helen Ruth Freeman, Katie Johntz, Martie McCleary Palar, Jayne Anne Phillips, and Jean Valentine.

And with thanks to Yerra Sugarman, whose wisdom has guided me on this and other paths.

By the rivers of Babylon, there we sat down, yea, we wept, when we
   remembered Zion.
We hanged our harps upon the willows in the midst thereof.
For there they that carried us away captive required of us a song; and
   they that wasted us required of us mirth, saying, Sing us one of the
   songs of Zion.
How shall we sing the Lord's song in a strange land?
If I forget thee, O Jerusalem, let my right hand forget her cunning.
If I do not remember thee, let my tongue cleave to the roof of my
   mouth; if I prefer not Jerusalem above my chief joy.
Remember, O Lord, the children of Edom in the day of Jerusalem;
   who said, Rase it, rase it, even to the foundation thereof.
O daughter of Babylon, who art to be destroyed; happy shall he be,
   that rewardeth thee as thou hast served us.
Happy shall he be, that taketh and dasheth thy little ones against the
   stones.

—Psalm 137

Don't suffer, poor soul, there is also for you something to be gained in
   this strange land.

—Medieval Turkish poem

Voyage

Imagine you lived
in a ravaged place, your house
shaking with the loud calls of rage
at uncontrollable forces, the calls
spilling into the street. And now
the house is gone, and during the long fire
that swept through the city
as a Hand dusts a table,
you were taken from the destruction and death
of those who knew you, and you labor among another people,
now, in their language, who feed you
from their bowls and also teach you,
on the leaf-strewn ground, their dancing. Still,
you cannot go home. When you look at the grasses here,
they are not yours; when you rest your forehead on the table
or run your hand over the bedding
that you lay in last night
with the one who holds you
wildly, carefully, these are not yours. It is possible that, if you
      displease,
if your voice does not lilt, anything could be taken from you.
Imagine that when you kneel down in the sand by the river
you see instead the ashes and bone chips
that are what's left of your people now, and when you try to
      hold
a handful to you, even that is merely the luminous green
river silt. You cannot remember their voices
under the river of other voices.
How then are you to sing in a strange land?

Walking in The Loop

Sometimes in a strong wind
she would call out to me
Walk backwards, and I'd turn
to face her, or I'd turn to flank her,
and the invisible force slapping my face
would finger my nape only.
It almost didn't matter that the other walkers
bent and faced forward.
My mother was helping me.

Thirty years later, Brian is telling me
about a woman he met, who was using
and has lost her kids. Relatives took them,
and though she's clean now,
no one speaks to her. The kids
don't want to come back. She wants to die. They know
she wants to die, but they don't
give a damn. Heartless,
is what Brian says. There's a 10-A.M. light
on his hair, issuing from the window
before which I married him. There's a terrible purity
in his opened notebook: a gaping white
laid upon the grain of his desk's stained eighty-year oak:
three generations of summer bands and winter bands.

In my fourteenth year, I left her. In my fifteenth year,
I worked at a hospital because I wanted to learn
how to help someone. She couldn't have known
I was there, bearing blood vials on another floor,
when they brought her in
to pump her stomach and tie her wrists, and, later, flood her
    skull
with those blazing pulses.

Mostly, I try not to look.

At her in the drowsy nest of the pills.
At her in the previous rage and despair, swallowing
  two by two: the choking and weeping the only sounds in the
  house.
At her sweating above me, all those years heaving my torso up
  and back onto the planks of the floor, as clay is thrown
  on a board, to soften it.
At her in the twist and release of voltage: wringing out a wash-
  cloth.
At her facing into the wind to watch over me
  that I not fall.

Also at myself not looking.

Limits and Proportions

He raped her once. He said, Cunt,
open your legs. At least
that's what her mother told me, years later. The dark bed
radiating dark. A bit of windowlight seeping in, and then
he would have padded back to the TV room, the swathed
    couch
he slept on while I came of age. Blue light
of old movies. Maybe she knotted the pillow
in halves or told herself
stories. The years
smeared with his oils, her rubbing furiously at them:
filth. seed. soil.

               *

He's just standing around, in a body shop;
wrenched engines groan
and fail. Substantial greased shadows
call out, they are like moving pistons,
they shine. Other cars, cakes on huge platters,
hover near the ceiling. My father's car waits, off-center, hood
agape. He's not looking. He
waits beside the car, but he won't touch it.

               *

The driveway tar sends the heat mist
back up, clear ripples lapping the engine block,
the rubber coils softened. The flesh of his back
is the coffee he takes in while shaving, is
the undulant froth he spreads on bread. What I want
is to touch him, hand him the appropriate screwdriver,
learn the syntax of repair. You're blocking the light,
he says. Now, I block the light often. I love
to block the light.

＊

The month before he left
my mother, we walked to the Holsum Bakery
Resale Shop. Two loaves of sliced enriched white
bread. Sixty-seven cents left over; a round woman
in a white bib apron; the sun
still coming up, the sidewalk flashing purple. Then
I took his hand. So quiet. With his thumb and forefinger
he rolled each of my hand's bones, maybe numbering them,
    maybe
naming them. I was twelve. Even if he's forgotten, once
he knew me.

＊

I only saw half of him. He opened the door partway
and stood sideways in the wedge, a rock forking the waters,
the past stream and the future, the inland river
and the terrible unbounded ocean. With his right hand he
    passed over to me
the black Hefty Cinch-Bag
of my belongings. Then held out his other hand. I was
sixteen. I put his housekeys
there. Dark pink palm, lined.

＊

May he sleep. May he dream an arm
cupping his head, the hard bowl of his skull. May the arm
    enclosing him
do so. May he sleep thus.

Tropism

This morning as I gave the ivy
a half-turn on the sill
so that none of the limbs
might falter, light-starved,

I remembered the other agony,
the aching turn toward the source,
each time I lie down
in bed with my mother
and try to touch her—

She's home from the ward. I've come back to her
just ripened, the first seeds
bursting from the stalk of me
as I lift the blanket and
gently

curve my form to hers. She's lying on her side.
I touch just her arm
—If only I'd thumbed the arc of the eyelashes,
if I had lightly grazed the down of her thigh,
even ah the sweet juncture of my mother's members—

She has so lately come from Death. Like the good child she
swallowed His pills, let Him feel a breast. How else
shall I win her
back to this world? How

but through my kisses on her calves
and wrists, each
motion of kiss forgiving a slap or a rending,
have I ever woken my mother back into
her body? But

when I stroke her shoulder
she edges away. Even now
this stuns me. Even now I want to
beg her
to shift a little closer, or pat my clutching hand.

Not to move away. Not to stir, look,
turn aside. Is my touch
so paltry, so
feeble? Did they lop her off at the very core?

There is nothing I can restore.
Since then, my bed is empty. Withered. Sere.

Fractals

Last night we watched them unfold
on TV: the intricate strictness
of a leaf, the formal rhythm of a cloud—
I love those discoveries that are not,
the variegated patterns which have been
beating just under the seventh layer
all along. Though also they terrify me,
because the red paisleyed structure of a mountain
comprises smaller paisleys, and so forth. Because
when I was six I buried my toy mouse who loved me,
so that she could no longer be taken away; to wrest her
from the territory of my mother's
vegetable shavings and sodden napkins, I thrust my beloved
under the planet's clodded surface. Because sometimes
Brian says *oh* and pulls my head into his furred chest,
as in when I said I buried her, and I hear his
valved and vesicled heart
open. Because each time sleep loosens him,
he's resting—pink of the ear, thick of the skull cage—
on my left wing of ribs
and then the ticking starts—no, not starts, *rises*—
and I hold him as his limbs unlock and I rock him
sometimes backward sometimes forward
because I can see where the fontanel has been
covered over and where the hoary rind will form
and his frame curl into itself and
later will shred and dissolve.
Because the design printed
on his seed is the shape of the rain
inside the rain, which tears down mountains and
builds them elsewhere.

How Miracles Work

In the eleventh century they would drape the girl saint
in her gold lace, set the tiara on her onyx head,
and process her, musically,
gravely forth, to the largest field. Then the mothers
would come with their crippled daughters blind sons raving
      mothers'
mothers, until the rains fell,
and the next day's damp, when the daughters
would lilt home, the sons
blink and return bearing firewood, the great-
grandmothers speak, or not, as was seemly. And in the morning
Brian came back to bed, clean-
shaven, his soles burning; it was time
for work but he handed me the salve
and then said nothing but
his breath. I don't know whether the children were healed. I
      don't
know whether the mothers of mothers
began again to live, or whether, after having been taken up
in my mother's arms and slammed against the planks of the
      floor
as a glazier smashes the flawed vessel, to re-
make me, so that I was nothing
but surface, perimeter and air, as Sainte Foy's skull
turns out to be a mineral shell
encasing a gasp,
space where the children of parents might decide to see
a veined light emanating,
I will ever love. Maybe
there's only surface, the bounds of flesh;
I felt so grateful for his
mild disease, the fine web of cracks in his skin
where I rubbed in balm, which

entered him, which healed him. And then,
slain again, the metal figure
on the plain, resonating
to the voices at the feast
at the edge of the woods.

The Fight

On the third day of the fight
that had begun over an apostrophe,
it was night in the room, he came in
dripping rain and not looking at me,
and we sat on the couch a long time
in the seventh month of our marriage,
and I had wanted to believe
some basic things about marriage—
not that it was a guarantee
but that it might at least increase the probability of
not being left, and that this other creature,
though also wracked, might spare me
a particular terror, an infinite terror: of un-
tetheredness. Think of the universe
expanding, which means stepping outside
itself, but outside is only
more it. You can see how those Iberians a few centuries ago,
for example, would rather watch a human burn,
twisting candlewick, than wander through the dark reaches
of starry shapelessness. Where is the Hand on the head? Where
    is
the Container of the fifty-six celestial spheres? So when he said
he didn't love me, and I sat beside him in the dark,
and my throat and lungs produced the howls like a dog's
    howls,
it wasn't about love, because how do I know what love is? it
    was
that he had put his fist through the surface of the skies.
And after that, nothing happened.

The Portent

Come look, he said, so I stood beside him on the doorstep
in the sharp night air, just as the other people stood,
in pairs and clusters, murmuring on their doorsteps,
and the traffic's red blinks, and feathers of mist
brushed the pavement, where in the morning the earthworms
    would lie fainting,
and he pointed into the sky—an invisible line
arced from his outstretched finger
toward the visible past, the candling lives of stellar bodies—
to show me that untethered moon tearing the sky
the way a needle parts the fibers
in its work of mending, the comet dragging
a little light in from the other side—

                                        And I could see
why they had trembled, in the last millennium, when the long-
    haired star
crossed their hearts' waters: There's so much
we don't know. For example,
whether the trail of light that marks the comet's
dying shows how we also,
struck loose, are shedding our substance as we go. Maybe
slightly burning.
When I took his arm then, he leaned into me
and I don't know if he was frightened, I don't know
whether he saw that great animate grief above us
as a warning, or whether he took comfort
from momentarily leaning against another
as we hurtle through space. But the neighbors were hushed
under their lamplights, and I could still see
those other figures,
clothed in skins, their few remaining spears
at their feet and their protector
fallen; they stood

heads tilted back, at the edge
of their country, and the sky torn
open: They were holding each other
by the waist and shoulder—for warmth,
and to steady each other
for the walk into the lost field.

The Admonishment

At the doorway of my life's
second half, I held up the sacred scroll
in its container, slightly tilted
as is commanded, so that the characters signifying
Almighty, King and Master and Creator, lean
toward the substance of the house, and then he
drove the nails into the doorpost oak—
I love that this requirement is
not a blessing; we weren't
sanctifying the beginning of our lives'
marriage: It is the holy warning we posted, that we be good
to one another. It's good, for example,
that as I held the mezuzah in its silver coat
up, he was careful to not hammer my thumb or index finger;
I admire that. My own hand
was shaking slightly, and I don't know whether
I could have managed to not
harm him, so deeply etched in me is the need
to wound, to dig my nails in, to leave my mark—after all,
that's the last thing I did before leaving
my mother, I could no longer speak
but I struck her
on her arms, her breasts, until she cried out
You hurt me! and then I was
released. But not released, because she cried out
and I was glad
as the serpent was glad, in his lithe flesh and
smiting wings, to see that naked pair
tremblingly flee through the eastern gate. Innocent children!
that they might finally learn,
from the stones on their bare soles
and the smoldering waves of their maker's
averted gaze, that their teeth rend, that their heels
grind and cause agony.

The Stave, the Tether

Sometimes at night he reads to me—
Rupert the Bear, Carla the Princess—
my head on his forested chest, his right arm crooked
around my waist, and we are entwined also at our thighs
and ankles: It is all I ever wanted, even when I could no longer
name it; I soak up, as the two-leaved plant takes in the live soil,
    his
lips at my forehead, the story
rumbling in his chest, and, beneath, the
pound and whisper, returning,
every time. The stories are similarly
about return: the bear in the end finding its lost dog, their joy
and relief. In this way, at the start of our marriage, he
mothers and fathers me; in this way he staves
my greedy four-limbed clutching: I prod him, for instance, and
    say
More story. More kissing, more heartbeat. Often,
he complies. Often, my throat swells up. So when I see,
over my shoulder, our child
hovering at the rim
of the lamplight, still not born, not made,
not held, not combed, not oiled, not lifted up, soothed,
    scolded, named,
and then grasp my husband by the shoulder bones
to pin him, to keep his gaze on me
because I am not done feeding, and then
lift my head to growl at that child, that she be warned
I am not slaked, this man is
my drink, my meat, no space for another
to feast at this board—I don't want to remember

that man from Judah, how he held the kid
around the slick ribs to steady her,
the tottering legs, the wiry haunch, how

he soaked a rag in milk and held it to her
long-lipped muzzle. The fronds of her lashes, the delicate
ear in the river of breath. How he led her mornings
to the succulent meadow and tethered her by his door
at suppers and in the mountain chill
the breath steamed from her nest of hay, and at the appointed
    day,
he led her with songs and chirruks
into the thorned wood because he was
full of sin—his appetite, his anger at his Maker—and he walked
    away
hearing her bleats and sobs. The terrified rustlings
in the brush as she tried to nose her way
home; the filmy eyes as the scented growls circled.

                                    It was never a casting-out
of stain, or an appeasement of the clenched Fist; it was
the rule of retribution: that the human also know
what it is to hear the loved creature weep
in fear in the wilderness.
That we might know what made us. Every year
the trembling flank, silk at the ankle, the ear flicking at your
    voice—
every year a similar beast. The same cry.

On my way home from teaching

The unwashed one on the subway
sits in a circle of peoplelessness;
there are the cool reflective seats and the steel poles
distorting the light, and he looks charred around the edges,
where you'd think there'd be pink: at the tops of the cheeks,
for example, or the border of the lips. And it's a sweet smell
sweeping before him like an arm clearing the table during a
    fight,
it's richly sweet, and humid, and you have to turn your head a
    little,
in the presence of death's hem, you have to avert your face.
—I would like to say that it was a holy stink, the way
they reported a scent of honey and attar rising from St. Alice's
    mouth
when she spoke her last sentences, on her pallet in the room
no one had dared enter for months, frightened by her
radiant disease, which she'd gotten from drinking the urine
and kissing the palms of lepers: the afflicted wanderers
about to be taken back. But
this wasn't a rose smell. And though I wish that
this man, narrow and thin-boned,
might be sacrificing his self for others, I worry
about how his eyes flicked when each passenger
shunned the seat beside him, how he bent his head when he
    was looked
at. I know how self-hate can be the best kind of Fuck-you.
As in the man who made me, who in his second marriage
again sleeps on the couch, who no longer bathes.
No one else will touch him,
so why should he. But the man on the subway
might have been wishing.—I know I can't know this.
And that it's easier to sorrow for the one who leaves
at Times Square, radiating that rot-smell which

really is the breath of swarming mites
chewing in the pores of human skin.
And because they batten on skin flakes, and multiply, and de-
    sire
to live, the demodex feast on the surface and the under-layers;
their gnawing that produces the sores on my father's sides and
    haunches
and on the other man now vanished
is also the marker that
the body is only partly ours,
these men bearing the flesh-eating colonies
not holy, I know, but they are earthly, they are still nourishing.

Lullaby

Even when he lays his sleeping head
upon my arm a long time, so that my arm
recalls its earliest life—its atoms calling out
to their starry origins—even when he comes home early
and drops the bags to open his arms more quickly, even though
he stood before me at the window
and intermingled his life with mine, I still know

he'll leave me. I can't shake it. Mostly, it's about
death, the moment when I'll press his eyelid with my lips
and it will not
tremblingly open. Half a millennium ago
they warned us about this: At the wedding
where Everyman was ringbearer, Mortal Death cheered vocif-
    erously
from behind the cake table. As though

anyone would need reminding. As though I hadn't seen
my grandmother stop wanting, when her beloved
began his long dissolve. His place at the table
looked heavy with transparence, just as
sometimes when I look at Brian from a distance
the air starts rippling like a flame's halo
between us: the universe issuing forth its reminders. For ex-
    ample,
the way it hardwires the human infant
to practice heartbreak, not allowing the baby to turn away
from the love always vanishing. Those howls.

Found Object

After the second fight, the one where
the novelty of fighting has worn off,
after I'd said *I don't like this* meaning *Come back* and
his face moved and looked like him again,

we walked around the neighborhood holding hands—it felt
   like swimming
because I was trembly from
what had been taken away—and we browsed
in the shops: The jars of olive paste at the deli
glowed plum-black; at the thrift store appliquéd cardigans
widened the weave of their stitches; and
in an upper corner a nappy beige teddy bear
looked just like a teddy bear, a paragon of teddy bear-
ness, so that I said *oh* when I saw it, and therefore Brian
reached into the corner, and drew it forth,
and gave it to me. I who have never understood
dolls and have scorned the little girls with their buggies
on Romper Room

answer the bear when it says *Where's the chocolate, momma?*
   or
Poppa doesn't have to go to work tomorrow, right? After a
   while
the bear privately reveals to me certain esoteric teachings—the
   Kabbalah of Bear—
on the nature of the amulet, the *bocio*
which stands in for the body
in order to become it, the bear
the thing that assigns us our forestalled names:
parent bears—the talisman that fills in for the real—

This is what wind is: One portion of air,
charged by the sun's pulses, grows light and flies up, and in its
vacated space rushes in
the weightier, the more substantial breath.

Yellow Sweater

On the way to the accountant
who will tell us
we don't have enough money
to have a baby, there's a small sweater
cloaking a fence stave, one of the arrowheads de-
limiting someone's property. It's a knitted thing,
sort-of white with yellow stripes,
about the size of a four-month-old,
and it's waiting for someone else
to make use of it. People do this,
in my new neighborhood: hang items on their front yards'
    boundaries
for other people to take. It seems to be
an organic response, a recycling,
on the principle of the universe, which,
in its economy of matter,
dispersed the pieces of its first-born stars
and re-formed the next generation from them, and thus
one or two shreds
of the cosmos's first gasp
wind up in each dense, mortal body, still wailing with the
    shock
of the cold non-light.

                    I think about those shreds now,
months later, when, in the hunt for the missing pillowcase,
I come upon the sweater,
its slack arms, its empty. How hungry our baby must be,
even unconceived, making its shadow cries
to be plucked up and attended to. And about the possibility
that it's not the aging chromosomal substance in its trailing
    half-lives
but the genuinely ancient material
of which we are partly composed

that starts shaking like a compass needle
in the direction of that sweater.

                            —Not that I believe in this nature idea.
After all, my mother, for example, swore that
because her body had made me, because my body fit within
    hers, because
I am formed out of her body's viscous stuff, she therefore
loved me. And really I was
another obstacle in her path of, her long labor of, dissolving.
And yet. Who heard,
when my father said they couldn't afford a child,
my pre-call? Enough to lie, and transgress, enough to punch
    through the membrane
of each condom, using a safety pin, the not-really-star-shaped
portals? Who couldn't help herself?

The Visitation

This time it happened at school: I shut the door
and looked at my desk and saw the papers spread out
as they would have been at her kitchen table—
its wood-grained round of vinyl pressboard, its rim
pocked from our fights—the table
where she was trying, in her fiftieth year,
to earn her real estate license. To help people pass plots of land
to one another. She was trying to live,
though she didn't want
to work. Though of course no one would have hired her,
because she talked to herself, because she
believed her own stories. Such as
the one where a doctor from the emergency room
has fallen in love with her and wants to marry her. Or her
    mother
sends her more money.
Such as the one where I come back and am sorry.
It's terrible to be left by the one you love; it's
terrible to survive. Under-live. The light is empty,
and my place at the table, and the house, and
she cries at the kitchen sink sometimes and throws things
at the place I've left. How
is it possible that the loved one has gone. I myself
try not to look.

                    Because even in the glowing haze
above my students' papers, she's reaching out for me. The gold
in her eyes. The arch of her tapered fingers. Because I am
practiced in leaving. Because in the knobby curves of my hands
    also
there is that which would drive away my own child. Just like.

The Messenger

At Columbus Circle there's a pigeon
in the station; it's rush hour and
people are walking barely around it—I myself
didn't notice it until almost
too late—the bird's hopping and peering and
flying a little way farther and back on the platform.
Red-throated. Mottled pearl. Last night

my subway line stopped so I left it
and found myself at Flatbush and Atlantic, and I should have
    been able
to find my way home but it was nine
in the dark and there were men and
I kept crossing Flatbush to look at the clock-tower
from different angles, and every way looked
wrong. Maybe the bird, trash dove, feels like that,
just a little—the jittering in each eye. It tries to fly
up when a train comes in and I know I'm being dumb but I
    worry
about whether it's panicking,
whether it wants to die. I know it's too easy

to worry about a bird, and how would I save a lost pigeon?
Come here, little bird? And the woman
on Lexington I walked past yesterday afternoon,
carefully organizing her shopping cart, whose jeans were
    stained
down the insides of her legs, who gave forth waves of sour—
how would I save her. Even my mother,
who utterly refused lithium and grew more
panicky more frantic more—I waited for her heart to stop
before looking inside
the house, before cleaning the stained
clothing, the stained favorite bedroom chair,

the filthed bowl. She could keep
nothing inside her, she was
that afraid. The cops who let me in through the yellow-taped
    unlockable door

later gave me her letters to them, in which she reported that
strange men broke in
and took her papers, that her ex-husband and daughter
wanted to hurt her, a midget named Frank wanted to—

that the Niles police might take care of her. And one of them
must have taken hold of the four-days-dead
calves and ankles, another would have shut off the shower
and held my mother's shoulders

too late. The bird flaps heavily from beam to beam,
faster when the second and third trains come in. Moses
    Maimonides said
there is an angel
enspiriting the seed
that it might form the limbs and breath of the conceived child,
and I would like to think he's half right, and that what Brian
    and I are choosing to want
is really the action of intelligences
lodged within our pelvic skulls.
I thought about calling Brian
to ask whether the bird will find its way out,
even though that's not the real question. No matter

how much I held her, my arms kept nothing
inside the container of her. When I walk past her on the street
    sometimes
part of me hates her: oh, yes, total projection. Another part
    hates
that I see only
my failure and not a woman reproving an empty shirt
for not staying folded. One eye looks at the left world,

one looks at the right, and then everything is flat
and there are twice as many dangers. For example,
wanting to rescue the bird.
For example, not wanting to rescue the bird.

The Sacrifice

I think the problem is, my first crush
was Mr. Spock. Specifically, I loved
his torment, composed of not having feelings
and having feelings: He worked
so hard against emotions, and when I was nine
I would sneak to the television after bedtime so that I might
    watch
the labor of holding oneself in.
And of course I would be
the one who with great effort and attention elicited
a response. It was gorgeous to imagine someone
quiet. I didn't think: *like my father,* or even
not like my ravishing
mother though of course it later turned out that every
    boyfriend
was slightly Vulcan. The ears were deceptively humanoid,
was all. Even now, I am drawn to the ways in which Brian is
absent. He doesn't worry, for example,
about whether I love him. He plays computer games, he types,
    he
turns his back to the room: I love
getting to drape myself over the turned back, getting to
    demand
the kiss—the turn toward, the lean
into. And then to get
the stopping, the turn again away. The two times
he's held on too hard, there has been in me a tinny blip
of horror: the vanishing dot on the screen, when you shut it
    off,
which lingers, brightly cringing. When I try to look away,
it's still there, glowing.

                                        That he might

want something from me.

                                        So it wasn't until we watched

The Ice Goddess
on PBS—the archaeologists in their parkas
hacking at the Peruvian snow, the child
they drew forth from the last millennium, huddled over his
    death,
his forehead pressed to the drawn-up knees,
the hands clutching the ankles as though he were still rocking
    himself,
the lips drawn up in that shriek. Nearby, his gold toy llama.
    Apparently
it was a privilege to offer one's child
up—the slaughtered boy's arms still holding very tightly
to empty space, and Brian not minding my weeping,
he himself moaning a little at the boy's broken skull—
                                                    only then
did I see how it might be, the boy wanting to be lifted up,
holding his arms out. Asking. Asking again.

The Measure

Lately I keep thinking about the man
whose shack burned away, on 112th Street,
who now has lost everything
except his two big dogs, who keep him safe,
and what will happen the next bitter night—
Possibly he will stay with them.
But then the next, the next,
and he will have to give in, or be taken somewhere—
gray ward, grid of cots—
and will have to imagine the dogs for years
waiting for him. Their plush muzzles, the grainy noses
scenting the air for him; their shivering
and then their lying down,
first the black one, then the black-and-brown,
still waiting. Even until the limbs stiffen,
until the eyelids stop
that flittering. What he tells Brian,
on Saturdays at the social-work site, is that he doesn't know
what to do. Last week Brian took him
a box of Milk-Bones, which of course is useless,
but the black dog licked his hand anyway,
not understanding that. How does anyone
take care of another. Brian says we can't fit the dogs
in our apartment, and he's right, but.
And Brian doesn't know about my not getting out of bed,
long ago, but there, the far wall. He doesn't know
how I want to conceive our Hannah or Joshua
and then recall the months I couldn't make rent;
that maybe I didn't want to.
What I let myself hope for lately
astonishes me. So it's hard to keep from
certain equations, however imprecise: such as,
I too could lose

everything. Still. We were making soup
when I said How old is he, and he
is thirty-seven, my age. And I remember looking
at the print we'd put up beside the sink, then,
of Michael, in his gilt-lumined armor,
who holds a balance for weighing souls: a rumpled little
    Casper-ghost
resting in the left-hand platter; the other descending, the
    draggled, cloudy shape there
with its arms cast up in its terror: Please don't. Please don't.
    The radiant
gold of the measure: As though there are reasons for hell.

Second Year

In the story of his life, Hitler said
he used to scatter crumbs on his barracks bedroom floor
for the mice, in the early mornings: "I had known
so much poverty in my life," he wrote
in his liminal cell, "I was well able
to imagine the hunger
and also the pleasure of
the little creatures," which is when
I put the book down on the quilt, seventy-six years later,
    Saturday,
sun on the bed, being lesser than a little creature
and confused. The apartment looks oddly hollow. Sometimes
it gets that way—cold tinge to its paint—and I remember I'm
    somewhere
leavable. When Brian's away, mostly; my former life
creeps into the future. As in, leaving the TV on
for the voices; as in bribing the resolute cat
to lie on me that I might sleep. So now,
in the second year of here, I have been trying to pay attention
to the neighbors' football shouts; to the boy in his new
    spectacles
who is practicing his two-wheeler,
steady up-and-down squiggles, in the street. I know
these people are not mine; I know someday Brian
may turn his back. But lately I've been training myself
to look anyway
at the trajectory's other side: This table, for example, may be
where I write a letter the week before I die. Brian's hand, more
    papery
but turning a page. And the egg that will drop down inside me
in four days from its stem the width of a straight pin
might be cared for, a Hannah or a Joshua
whom I would possibly succeed in

not damaging. I have been allowing myself
to feel grateful. I have been schooling myself thus. To think,
my life has changed. And now I might even
be capable of putting down a book
to wearily push a pull-toy
without pinching or leaving or reproach. However,
Hitler also imagined himself finally safe, a good person,
desirous of giving
back. It doesn't matter
that the parallel's false. Even if he'd once risen
from the chill corner and seen
he was really feeding himself,
he would still have had to have
his hatreds. I know. What I don't get is
how I could have gone on until now longing for safety, how
     could I
even now be practicing the feel of relief. It is a dangerous thing,
     isn't it,
to love one's life, to lay the book on its open face
and bend back the spine at the crease
because you can't bear it and because
it's time to start supper, there are the mottled glossy
potatoes to dice. There is the risk of seeing
the blade parting the grainy curtain
to let in more of that wet light. There is the risk
of thinking you see this.

The Virtue

Today at breakfast I looked at Brian—
the wisps of his eyebrow hairs,
the way he licked the spoon
after he stirred the milk into his tea,
and I could hear my father
under the voice of the spoon clacking against the cup,
who would direct one accusing index finger at me
as a vector finds its only course to the originating plane,
and, swiping the other index finger over it—swish of a
    pendulum—
would look at me and say Shame. How dare you
judge a book by its cover. Thin, sad sentence. And now I feel
partly grateful that I have been so schooled
as to look at my bespoused and see how he sits
alone at the table,
how he goes on reading through the cloud of tea-steam,
how I will never know what he tastes,
or reads, or cries out for, some nights.

Exile

When Ezekiel saw the four-faced ones,
he kept looking. The creatures
came forward in their mighty wings
which brushed the likeness of the rising firmament,
and he kept looking
higher: the likeness of the throne, glowing,
and then what seemed to be the figure of a human,
which was the Glory, loins and shoulders and neck—
And Ezekiel saw and
threw himself down on the soil, one forearm across his eyes,
the other shielding the back of his head,
and over his own broken chanting the plush hum of wings,
and above these, the Voice—

Maybe he covered his eyes and trembled
out of fear. It's important that the ground
was not his homeland, and yet the Voice was of there. Maybe
    he shook
out of joy, or great grief
at his unworthiness. Yesterday when I came home, there was
    late sun
in the kitchen, the neighbors' kids playing ball in the backyard.
Our supper plates still in the sink
looking already washed, from the sun,
and the wings inside my chest
opened—

        It might have been shock and relief,
because I have still just burst through
the front door and run to the park two blocks away
where my mother will not follow
even to claim her bleeding child. It might have been
joy: that I have been made

to see that light in the window, to press my ear against the left
    wing
of Brian's rib cage—its *shush, shush*—as I used to tightly clutch
my mother, when nothing was happening. She gave me her
    thick body
to hold, she gave me everything she was. I'm not saying
she was the glory or the appearance of the glory.
I'm saying I slid down to the floor and held my head
that I might not see
the crease inside her shoulder,
where I used to press my face. Who gave this to me,
who else taught me to clasp my full length to the other:
even waiting for the voice in its terrible shouting,
and the wings in their frenzy and riot,
even then to pay attention, to hold on.

Proleptic

Sometimes in the dream someone's trying to kill me,
or me and Brian but Brian's not paying attention
and I have to worry whether he's left clues—
in the less-dreamed life,
at the cusp of my third year with him, I notice sideways
an absence of pain: the four-in-the-morning air
husky with snoring, the odd grumble at a cat-romp;
and even awake he doesn't turn away. Sometimes I notice
I'm not noticing, which is also a good thing.
Though I think it is my bounden duty
to look carefully at these kindnesses. That we use one tooth-
    brush,
for example; that he doesn't mind not having separate
towels. That at night his right leg heavily overleafs my left,
and I don't frantically slowly run from the dreamed dangers;
    instead,
I try to figure them out: How can I keep us alive?

Last week at the museum there were icons from the holy city
    of Byzantium:
jeweled storied chalices,
and in a side room carved ivories you could fit in your hand to
    pray with—
these were plain, creamy mineral, minutely figured
by ancient chisels, and in one, of Mary's Dormition,
her family history gathered around the bed—the Visitation at
    bottom right,
Elizabeth's hand on her belly; the manger; at the top left,
the Pietà, which is the pain accompanying love—the central
    Mary's
face and neck and shoulders were a stone smudge
because she had been worn down
from daily kissing. Which is all I have ever wanted.

Rain on the Roof

One night I kept waking up
with this ballooning feeling in my throat
and shoulders, a warmth romping in me
the way the cats sometimes vault
through the rife dark—I couldn't stay asleep
because the door in my chest kept flying open.
And Brian lay there, curved spine,
quietly radiating, so that I could press my face against the
    amber
frothed-honey heat of his ribs and then he'd lean
slightly into me, a ship riding the rolling ocean belly,
and I would be weighted down,
the way you put a plate on the extra shirt
so it won't blow down the hill—
I think it was happiness. At least
that's what I kept telling Brian
with every billowing-up from sleep: I feel so
happy. Though I don't know what to call it,
really. Mostly I am a groveler. I love you so much, mama,
I would say, bringing her her root beer
sizzling in its glass, dish of ice cream, the pearly peach
nail polish bottles. There are letters
I left under her pillow, with drawings of a mother and daughter
under a boundless sky, which was how much
I loved her. I said it, there is
proof. I fell for it myself, forgetting again
I'd meant only to ravish and content her. Similarly
I bring Brian his cups of tea,
rice pudding. To greatly please him
I pack his lunch. And I don't know if that's okay
because I suspect us.
And him, and me. So, sometimes it's a relief
to give up purity. Which may be what they taught me

when, for instance, they took the training wheels
off my bike, and I fell and fell,
shamed—the concrete, the crushed grass—and then my mother
held the handlebars and my father held the back fender
and we flew
down the hill, the three of us,
and my mother fell away
from the speed and my father was calling out
I've got you, keep going, I've got you,
and at the end, he
hadn't been there. And this was
how to live. How to rise up.

Sunday, May 30, 1999

After we came home from errands,
we made supper, and I read the e.p.t. box
over salad. Brian had put bits of bleu cheese
and bright carrot in it, and I remember
reading the part about "only 3 minutes for a response"
just when I thought to tell him how good the Saga was,
and for a second not knowing which to say first.
And later, I peed on the e.p.t. stick,
which soon may not embarrass me to say, when
larger chunks of my day are devoted to the acts of the body,
and then I sat there, on the edge
of the tub, and looked. The lavender stripe
lifted up from the blank white
the way a face emerges from the developing pan,
so that finally you can look at the person
all you need—It was like
looking down from a great height, like in that scene in *Vertigo*
where Jimmy Stewart stands on a stepladder
and the vast space below him
writhes to shake him loose,
because at that point in the story he loves
no one. It's terrifying to be alone in the world,
and it's no help knowing we all are, even
Brian, and I, even the forming embryo. So I sat on the cast-iron
    rim
and let the floor wobble for a second. After all, at the beginning
of the day, I'd felt that wobble: I was setting out the plants
on the fire escape, Brian handing me
first the massed aloes, then the heavy-branched jasmines,
the ivies, and it was when I was trying to place the littlest pot,
    of sage,
safely on the grate
so it wouldn't tip over between the bars,

that I saw the garden three stories below
rise up and recede and rise, and I held on
to the rust-flaked rail and then got onto my knees
because the world had changed, or hadn't,
because he loves me, or doesn't, and
still. No one can keep me from
myself, from what I could do without thinking.
Such as, leaping into the next life. Causing harm.

Eighth week, driving home after the sonogram, Beethoven

pouring into the car, the East River
fiercely gleaming, the string section leading the horns
as we take that curve where the bridges appear,
first the blue Manhattan, then the arcing Brooklyn,
all of us in that surge, and in me a heart
is beating, I saw it
flicker on the screen the way a star issues out
into the night sky, in those huge pulses that emanate
what we live on. And then it's that place
where the horns are seriously pounding,
and for a moment I almost turn
to the back seat,
to see whether the baby is liking these sounds: the horns
pushing into the exit lane, the central line of flute
in that billowing joy, and the strings hurling themselves
forward, yes, I want to tell her-him, the music opens up
in your chest, it's supposed to feel
a little painful. Though it's too soon to explain
the grief of the man
who wrote down this music
because someone he'd loved, someone he'd thought would save
    people,
turned out to be cruel. So that really
the music pushes forward
through a curtain of pain like an atmosphere rippling
above a fire. It's like those movies where the astronaut
leaves Earth, the capsule shaking
to show how we could shatter,
and the astronaut's face blurring
as though his accumulation of sorrows were finally
falling away. That's what's happening here
in the car, so I speed up over the bridge

to mark it, and because the music is surging, and the second
    heart inside me,
and when I looked in the rearview mirror
just now, the back seat was empty
but wasn't. Because really I am
the space capsule, the shuddering vehicle, and whatever those
    sorrows
my baby is moving toward—even the ones I make—
for a little while, this rider, this star-creature, fellow Earthling,
is spinning itself inside me.

Twelfth week, sixth day,

five A.M.: The crows woke me up,
and when, dazed with sleep, I looked for them,
there was a moment
when I couldn't tell that I was looking, not out,
but at my reflected eye. The alien glitter, there,
which signals volition, like the birds' avidity
for anything edible. What
will my child see in me? Lately I have flashes:
I can see I'm about to move out of danger; death's gleaming
    feathers
have not brushed the still-webbed hand
fluttering inside me. But also I am moving
into danger, curling tighter beneath the piano bench
as my mother walks away, still heaving. I hope
you never have children, she calls out from the kitchen,
and then she says, No, I hope you have someone just like you,
then I would see what it's like, having a child who
reads on her bed all day, jumps wildly on the bed
so that she might soar past the ceiling, wants,
wants. Even now, part of me wants
a mother I could call up to tell, Mama, my skirts don't fit, and
I'm afraid I won't want to take care of a baby, and
how the hell do you wash it?—And the slick fish-child turning
    within me
wants, ferociously, also, wants drink and meat, wants
the very air my body contains.
It's a good thing, though,
isn't it, to feel
want. I partly loved seeing her in stores, watching
how she stood, leaning toward the brightest boxes. That
nervous shift from foot to foot,
as though she were rocking herself. How she needed me then
to block the cameras, the sharp-necked mirrors,

which I tried to do
artfully, while she slipped a pretty cup and saucer
in her handbag. To shield her
with my body, from the world's
view of her. What she could not see
in herself was the me in her—that greed, that sucking mouth—
and I will meet her again,
soon, my long-lost, my beloved.

The Message

Just before supper there was a plucking on the strings
of the window screen, which turned out to be
a chipmunk, ravenous for the crusts I'd left on the sill.
It was splayed, its pale belly pressed to the steel mesh, it was
a writhing tube of fur, it was clipping wildly
a portal with its teeth,
that it might wriggle through
to the other side. This action I recognized instantly: to devour
what you desire. I myself started
early, in that regard, grabbing
maraschino cherries from the jar
because they looked like drinks, like escape,
and womanhood. Except,
they were only there for the Bachelor-Button cookies my
     mother baked
to show me she was a mother, so their disappearance
signified a gap in the symbol's center. Sometimes I think my
     mother
was loved by her mother
too much. Too thoroughly. If only my mother had feared
displeasing her adorer, she might have feared
harming me. But my mother's mother
did accepting things: In the flyleaf of *The Joy of Cooking*
is written For my daughter,
who is a mother now. It's the sort of message
I'm a sucker for, the way it holds out its arms.
Not that I know what the words mean—
what is this "mother" category, for instance? Did she become a
     mother
when I first pummeled her
from the inside? When she soaped very carefully the top of my
     head,

making circles with her fine hands? When she held me by the
    ankles
to drag me down the yellow carpeted stairs, my ridged skull
knocking like a metronome? When I shouted from outside, I
    hate you,
so that she drew in her breath and turned away, weeping? How
does one mother some separate creature in its isolating pelt?
How will I keep myself from
the one who is turning within me? When really
what I love is to take
the man's cock inside me before I'm ready,
so that it hurts, so that
he tears me, slightly, open.

Imago

Frankly, the thought of something coming out of my nipples
horrifies me. It's this idea I have

about intactness: I want my body
sealed. Or, I think of the body

I inhabit as a sealed thing, the container
of me. Long ago I deduced

the me and the body
were separate entities, my mother in a square of sun

astraddle and shaking my body,
as one shakes dirt from a rug, though

crying and blood-suffused from
the look I'd given her, from my refusal to

speak. Which I continued, practicing
as I gazed at her

eyes' flecked amber, her Russet-Red hair undulating in the air,
the long-branched veins of her neck

delivering sap over the course of her—
an anti-maple tree—

above the drum-noises
of my head knocking against the floor

I'd think, It's just my body;
she can't get

Me. As in, she can't make me come out
from the container. Think of a pupa

fleshily waving from its pale cocoon.
Or that *X-Files* scene, where the black oil,

the essence of intent, forces its human host
to his knees, that it might

go home. And now the me will be leaking out,
pouring, apparently, onto the unscented material world,

as well as into the being now amplifying itself into actuality, in-
    side me.
Sometimes, though, I wish I could hear that magnifying whir

of the fetus, meaning *little one,*
its swallows and sighs. And though it's just my body

producing the infant, it does so with such
animal devotion, weaving each filament so as to ornately span
    the gulf in the forest.

And it's my body, the arms and shoulder-sockets,
that throbs, that craves

to clasp that naked being to me, back and forth, back and forth.

The Present

I loved how, when we filed into the room,
it was already dimmed, like when you walk into a movie late
and everyone's chatting because there's about to be
a story, only for once I wasn't late—
                              the instruments glowed, and
   the blue-
swathed table, and also the warmed jelly they daubed on my
   abdomen,
a fizzy green the color of the lifeblood of those *X-Files* aliens
who want to take shelter on Earth.
                           Then the screen

blinked. And there was the creature
who has begun inside me. First we saw knees, their formal
   curves
like the ogees at the tops of windows in holy places.
Legs curled, uncurled, and this created one revealed
the bud of the penis, joining the lower limbs of a
him, which is when I had to look away for a moment,
to press my hand on Brian's face, his lips and throat, a wild
   startlement
fluttering inside me, as the generations
of my family's women and their girls
unlocked their linked arms
to deliver me from their circle.
                    I think Brian smoothed the
   length of my fingers
against his neck-pulse. Meanwhile, the baby boy, child of my
   right side,
having burst from my right ovary and clung to the closest place
all this time, was turning
away and toward, stretching and nestling. And then
he reached out—his hand
opened, like a fireworks blooming in the night sky,

or like a sea anemone pinkly moving
to grasp the pearly morsel
that's drifted, ah, near, or
like a baby Cortez reaching for the ultra-
sound-saucer's presence pressing faintly into
his place of shelter.
Like God, who, before He buried His Moses
and fell silent,
brought Moses to the peak of Pisgah and opened His Hand
over the vast lands of Gilead,
the strange green of the unknown. And the human creature
looked—his eyes might have stung from the glitter,
after four decades in the wild sands—as the Hand,
the fine-grained Palm and the five rayed Fingers,
swept over the expanse, to say Behold
the future.
      —Though the doctor said, Look.
He's saying, 'Hi, mom.'

On Empirical Evidence

I don't know anything. It's a problem.

I, I, I, I. It's always about me, isn't it.

As in, why did I want to have a baby? What if I just missed my
    old fight
against erasure? As in, the lesson will turn out to be:
Let go a few I's, and the one speaking now says, Not a chance.

                                When Brian yells at the cat
    for midnight-jumping,
I mean really yells, and with his foot caves in the sides of the
    wastebasket
with two echoing bursts, then slams the door
in possibly disproportionate cat-banishment,
one I cowers in rage;
one I thinks Baby
will learn this kick-cower dance.
Oh, good, that I thinks. That is, as they say,
rich. Well-chosen, Sharon.
Another I bides awhile and then approaches
the exiled creature, who has stationed itself at the door
for the long dumb night of the soul. When I stroke its silken
    flank and throat and ear,
it shifts away. The longing is to drape oneself, chin and neck,
    upon
the ankle of the feared one. Yes, the I blinks, recognizing this.

I don't know how most stories end. Or
what any story is from inside someone else's I.
So I try to be careful: e.g., whose longing for the ankle?

Sometimes such longings horrify me. I wanted a baby
a) to hold another creature, gurgling, up to the light, which

I have lately found abundant; b) to remedy old wrongs; c) to be
curled up beside. Taking, taking.
                                        The one thrumming
        inside me
will form his own versions.

I know only a few endings. The puppy
snaps at the seven-year-old's experimentally tormenting finger,
        and therefore the father
kicks the animal, auburn plush rib cage arched up and
thudded into the wall. And again. Not much sound
but a slight whine. The eyes, though, the dog's eyes
full of love.

Of course I watched. How could I not
want to see my own plot elements
replayed in oh slow motion.

It's the old wrong, and I don't know if I wanted to right it
or watch it again.

In the daylight Brian says sorry and
un-dents the wastebasket. Which is, after all, inanimate. Maybe
        shifts occur

in generations as in tectonic plates. Old knowledges
get unexplained. William of Conches said that a seed would
        form a male child
if implanted in the womb's right side, because the liver, nearby,
gave off a purifying heat. Half a millennium later,
my baby boy has nested his entire gestational term
on my right side, my belly bulging visibly fuller there, because,
because

Notes

"The Fight"

The philosopher Giordano Bruno (b. 1566) asked, "What would happen if you put your hand through the surface of the heavens?" For positing that the universe is infinite, Bruno was arrested by the Inquisition in Venice, imprisoned for seven years in Rome, and burned in the public square on February 17, 1600. Aristotle believed there were fifty-six celestial spheres. See Evry Schatzman, *Our Expanding Universe,* trans. Isabel A. Leonard (New York: McGraw-Hill, 1992).

"The Portent"

"The long-haired star" is a name given to Halley's Comet in the Anglo-Saxon Chronicles, 1066 (the year that William of Normandy conquered England).

"On my way home from teaching"

St. Alice of Schaerbeek (d. 1250); see Martinus Cawley, ed. and trans., *The Life of Alice the Leper* (Lafayette, Oreg.: Guadalupe Translations, 1987).

"Found Object"

"Bocio" means "empowered [bo] corpse [cio]" in Beninese; it is a sacred object with magical properties. See Jacques Mercier, ed., *Art That Heals: The Image as Medicine in Ethiopia* (New York: Prestel, in association with the Museum for African Art, 1997), 9–15.

"On Empirical Evidence"

William of Conches wrote in the twelfth century. See William F. MacLehose, "Nurturing Danger: High Medieval Medicine and the Problem(s) of the Child," in *Medieval Mothering,* ed. John Carmi Parsons and Bonnie Wheeler (New York: Garland, 1996).

University of Central Florida
Contemporary Poetry Series

Mary Adams, *Epistles from the Planet Photosynthesis*
Diane Averill, *Branches Doubled Over with Fruit*
Tony Barnstone, *Impure*
Jennifer Bates, *The First Night Out of Eden*
George Bogin, *In a Surf of Strangers*
Van K. Brock, *The Hard Essential Landscape*
Jean Burden, *Taking Light from Each Other*
Lynn Butler, *Planting the Voice*
Cathleen Calbert, *Lessons in Space*
Daryl Ngee Chinn, *Soft Parts of the Back*
Robert Cooperman, *In the Household of Percy Bysshe Shelley*
Rebecca McClanahan Devet, *Mother Tongue*
Rebecca McClanahan Devet, *Mrs. Houdini*
Gerald Duff, *Calling Collect*
Malcolm Glass, *Bone Love*
Barbara L. Greenberg, *The Never-Not Sonnets*
Susan Hartman, *Dumb Show*
Lola Haskins, *Forty-four Ambitions for the Piano*
Lola Haskins, *Planting the Children*
William Hathaway, *Churlsgrace*
William Hathaway, *Looking into the Heart of Light*
Michael Hettich, *A Small Boat*
Ted Hirschfield, *Middle Mississippians: Encounters with the Prehistoric Amerindians*
Roald Hoffmann, *Gaps and Verges*
Roald Hoffmann, *The Metamict State*
Greg Johnson, *Aid and Comfort*
Markham Johnson, *Collecting the Light*
Hannah Kahn, *Time, Wait*
Sharon Kraus, *Strange Land*
Susan McCaslin, *Flying Wounded*
Michael McFee, *Plain Air*
Judy Rowe Michaels, *The Forest of Wild Hands*
Richard Michelson, *Tap Dancing for the Relatives*
Judith Minty, *Dancing the Fault*
David Posner, *The Sandpipers*
Nicholas Rinaldi, *We Have Lost Our Fathers*

Sharon Kraus's first book of poems, *Generation,* was published in 1997. An earlier version of *Strange Land* was selected as a 2000 finalist in the National Poetry Series. Her poems have appeared in *TriQuarterly, Agni, The Georgia Review, Prairie Schooner, The Massachusetts Review, Quarterly West, Barrow Street,* and other journals. Her awards include fellowships from the Mac-Dowell Colony, the Bread Loaf Writers' Conference, and the Squaw Valley Writers' Conference; the Editors' Choice award from *Columbia: A Journal of Literature and Art;* an Academy of American Poets first prize; and a National Academy of Arts and Letters regional first prize. She teaches at Queens College, City University of New York.